Shots From A Passing Car

by ron vazzano

Domenica Press

1322 2ND ST. SUITE 24 SANTA MONICA, CA 90401

Requests for permission to make copies of any part of the work
should be mailed to:

Domenica Press
Attn: Permissions
1322 2nd St. Suite #24
Santa Monica, CA 90401

www.domenicapress.com

ISBN 0-9746482-0-5

Library of Congress Control Number: 2004092221

Printed in the United States of America

Acknowledgments:

Cover illustration and frontispiece: Chris Gall
www.chrisgall.com

Art Director / cover design: Jeff Weekley
jweekley@mac.com

Grateful acknowledgment is made to each of the following publications, anthologies and other media outlets in which these poems first appeared: "The Fledgling" in *Bone & Flesh*; "A Death In The Family" in *Daybreak*; "The Pawn" in *Echoes*; " '52 Cards" and "A Return To Yankee Stadium" in *Fan*; "Ants Across The Acropolis" a contest winner on *www.HugoBoss.com*; "Winter Street" in *Icharus Falling*; "Nine men stand waiting…" (haiku) in *Line Drives: 100 Baseball Poems*; "Jackie On Third" at the LIU sponsored Jackie Robinson 50th Anniversary of his "Breaking the Color Line" Commemorative in 1997; "Tin (A Tenth)" read on KUSC in Los Angeles; "Stale Mates" and "The Third Avenue El" in *the new renaissance*; "Out Back" in *Standing On The Ceiling: (An anthology of poems on the joys and sorrows of being a parent)*; "On A Smoking Break" in *Prairie Winds*; "Buddies" in *THEMA*.

Special Note: The author has published most of his previous work under the name *Ron Lawrence* prior to returning to the legal use of his original name: *Ron Vazzano*.

Artwork Credits: *Original Illustration/Painting* or *Adaptation*: Jeff Weekley pages 14, 33 (Charles Dodgson Archive), 39-41, 91; Ron Vazzano: pages 36, 44, 45, 63, 77, 100, 105; Almie Vazzano: page 145; *Original Photo/ Reproduction* or *Adaptation*: Ron Vazzano: pages 45, 51, 57, 61, 133, 139, 149; Almie Vazzano: page104; Michelle Vazzano: inside flap bio photo, page 147, Sal Randazzo: page 136; Vazzano Family Archives: pages 119, 149; *The New York Times* Archives: page 7; *The Topps Company, Inc.* (original card ownership: Ron Vazzano) page 94; Public Domain Archives: pages 81, 114-115, 124, 125.

The author would especially like to thank Michelle Vazzano for her contribution as proofreader and Jeff Weekley for offering his artistic talents far beyond the call of duty, to make this book become a reality.

for Michelle, Almie and Dylan with all my love

C●ntents

I. At The Wheel

II. Sort Of True Confessions

III. The Lamplight Glowing

IV. Just Business

V. They

VI. Scenes

VII. La Famiglia

Shots From A Passing Car

"How foolish his aim had been!"

James Joyce, *A Portrait Of The Artist As A Young Man*

I. At The Wheel

"...any turn in the wheel of sensation has the power to crystallize and transfix the moment upon which its gloom or radiance rests..."

Virginia Woolf, *To The Lighthouse*

Squirrels Making Bad Decisions

The animal instinct so acute—
these cute little animals
ought to know better.

Or so it would seem.
                    And yet they dart
with such precision— *precisely*
at the wrong moment—

across the road.
Some even stopping in mid-dash and thereby
compounding the error of their ways.

Then retracing their scurried steps
                                   eyes wide open
                                       noses
feverishly twitching
                    ears wired for sound

they forego the concept altogether
of being past the point of no return.
And given options, they tend to return

to the road
                or to be more precise
to that side of the road most traveled by;
where cars like comets come hurtling by.

Their rocket scientist fathers
having since moved on
to their own bad decisions
                        whereabouts unknown

perhaps a pelt left strewn across
some double yellow line
have nothing to teach in the matter.

And proper nutrition left to the mother—
she knows nothing of speed and oncoming cars.

The only sense of safety here
lies somewhere in the numbers.
Which they throw at the world
with reckless abandon.

Free Verse

Frost, frugal
      with patience

for those who might put up
walls of stone between us

      nevertheless

insisted upon the need for a net.

A far less-seeded poet wonders why.

Is not the volley between ourselves
and the shadow of how great
we can become?

Shots From A Passing Car

Mise-en-scène... Monday morning:
Windows rolled down; odometer rolled up—

A thousand light years on the sly—
Fifth-and-Fifty-Fifth at Pentameter Square

Passing by the Metaphorical Museum of Oz;
Across from the Avenue of Alliteration.

In rapid transit transformation
Lines run from head to toe

On laundry tickets and AMEX receipts
For lunches long digested— loose pens

And all forms of scrap paper gathered
From the glove compartment like guns and ammo.

Just one more morning with the night job packing heat.
Outside, joggers, deaf to Brubeck pounding

On a CD like a heart inside the chest of my car—
An arrhythmia tracking in five-fourth's time—

Jog in their swell shoes in a semi-sort of rhyme.
Their pace, a metronome of modest arc;

Soles at one with the pavement in measured strides.
My car continues careening, cutting corners;

Crashing into syntax— running red the lights and signs
In a gangster attempt to get away—

The shots from within ringing out mostly missing.
Then from the blind spot in the mirror, a cop appears.

He asks to see my poetic license.
Then blocks off the right brain with a string of orange cones.

Which of course sets the wheels of wonder to melting.
Which in turn reconnect to that stretch of common tar;

That black river flowing with the go.
He lets me off with one last warning.

The Pawn

Observe the halo about its global head;
the sharp lines and gray wash of shadow spun
in bell-shaped curves to its base.
A carving in utility, it cuts a noble swath:
humble, majestic, warrior fierce.
From its post sending ripples in resilience it begs
no grand plan of itself
but to hold.
To hold in belief that they who stake claim
to the central squares
will see The Plan unfold and dance
like deadwood resurrecting.
That the work of the Wood-pusher depends as much
on the wood as the hand to move it along.

Ants Across The Acropolis

Here where no rivers flow from open wounds
and spleens remain unvented;

where broken hearts must have called it a day
(gone deep sea fishing off the Cape of Good Hope?);

where no male enclaves find themselves
slipping on a *zanana* peel
no pundits licking their ice cream koans
(with a "K") on talk-show clatter,

I pause to follow a battalion of ants
making their way
across the Acropolis.

In their hustle-bustle line of worldly oblivion,
and my entrancement
with purpose, so Lilliputian—

it drives the Greek gods crazy.

I try to point out that ants,
more or less,
are the same the world over. Their Olympic Games
would all end in a draw.
Their 26 inch marathon, while rolling a pebble
of size and scale to turn Sisyphus green
would all be over in under a minute.

This, of course, would allow them
ample time to get back to their work
never stopping
to consider themselves.

Penmanship

The nuns believed good penmanship
was next to God
                    and so I practiced
the Palmer Method.

Over and over and over
  I'd go
winding my way through
that slinky of "O's";
                    then jumping
up and down
and up and down
in a field of wheat
  of stalks of lead —
blunting my small pencil —
I aimed to get it right.

Exactly when the "Q's" and "P's"
became so full bellied
so sure of themselves —
I can't quite recall.
It may have been just before the fall
  of '63

maybe when the signature interlocking
  "th" became mine;
something that still defines me —

though the definition itself remains
  like Amelia Earhart —
missing.

The "f" picked up its flourish
  and particular tail
somewhere along the trail to manhood —

a steeplechase over
spasms and desire.

And the "S's" perfect
impersonation of a snake
was impromtu
                    but binding;
hissing at all
that crosses its way.
Till this day.
Till this day.

To loop or not to loop
the lower case letters?
                    Depends
it seems

on the given time
and space allotted.

And as stars and dreams have slipped through
    the hour glass—
that fine line between
the top and bottom—

and the peacock has taxied
out of Gotham

the loops have all but gone away.
Along with the dotting
of every "i".

The Cherry Horses

Is it that we have
        But one summer, one chance
To ride the cherry horses
        In their calibrated circle?

Remember how they had bared their teeth
        At the pull on the reins?
How they glistened in their paint?
        You can almost hear them whinny

In that callioped syncopation—
        Heads bobbing up and down
To a summer's lost tune
        To a fool heart's delight.

There were no dreams to cling to in that ride
        Of what was or might one day be.
Just a present and perfect circle of moment.
        The one we now hold to the autumn light

On a pedestal of fingertips.
        But have no fear.
We dare not let it fall.
        No, we dare not let it fall.

Hear the music box begin
        See the circle re-spin.
Ride again
        The Cherry Horses.

I Keep This Journal In Lieu Of Keepsakes

I've passed the mid-point in my story:
the fulcrum upon which life sits in the balance

to catch its breath between the stages.
Note the exposed string that ties it all together

in the binding of this book I bought in Venice...
this year? Last? A millennium ago?

The birthdays alas have outlived the cake;
the simple song; the pointed hats

and most of all the wish-blown candle.
My pen is my candle now, with which

I mark my wishes; make my days.
I keep this journal in lieu of keepsakes

in lieu of the ubiquity of souvenirs—
the snow globes circumnavigated;

the key chains too plastic to hold even a key
to the tiniest door much less The Big Gate;

the T-shirts with their iron-on icons of cities—
I do this to remind me not so much of where I've been

but what was on my mind while I was there.
And there but for the grace of God went I:

never helpless, homeless nor haunting the streets—
I brought home the bacon in the very absence of a pig;

forsaking the golf shots while shanking the lamb.
I savored the sizzle along with the steak

then made love with my conscience;
shared a smoke with my id.

I took shelter in the book stacks on sweltering days
then went out to go swimming in the hurricanes.

Spalding Gray was my favorite color;
black & white— clear-cut: my least.

I've come lately, Johnnie, to see me in all my tenses;
some something less, than pluperfect, for sure.

I've watched myself upstage myself—
flash in the pan; steal my own thunder;

I've pummeled my poems— to what point?— with my puns;
gone maudlin on mandolin— damn my tin ear.

I've sung a tune of myself only a dog could hear.
I've come to prefer the company of cats.

A snail trudges by.
It leaves wet spots in its wake.
They dry up quickly.

Xmas Tree

Freshly cut and carted off
to say, Any County, USA

this Douglas Fir
might be said to be dying.

To be or not to be is not
an option for the designated tree.

Yet in its severed and uprooted state
it clings to itself
by the will of its very own branches;

summons up the plasma reserves
of its own sweet sap;

glories in its own
delicious essences.

How long denied of mother's milk
and God's green earth
could you go on?

A question perhaps for St. Thomas Aquinas.
For even the headless chicken quickly
runs amok and out of time.

But the tree stands tall. Uncomplaining.
A miracle in the making
in your own living room,

it keeps guzzling water
from the bottom up
    while weighted down

with our baubles and beads
and bubbling lights.

One less noble would have long ago yielded
to the Ghosts of Yuletides past
at the very first whack
of the woodman's axe.

But the tree, like Christ
hangs on.

On Pumpkin Time

In the midst of it all
the pumpkin gets carved.
The loose membranes—
stringy, tissued, mucus lined;
the consistency of life
and its afterbirth—
the candle set down
like a headstone.

Kinetics On Mott Street

The click and clack of balls beneath
the low hung shade

the mattress of smoke
the green felt meadow

where worlds collided
energy transported

forces and motions
worked on the masses;

directions changing—
it could go

either way.
Every shot.

The laws of Physics 101
played out here between

the mahogany rails
and inlaid diamonds

in mother-of-pearl;
the geometric

reference points
for bank shots,

boundaries,
misspent youth.

The upstart denizens
strut with their cue

massaging their tips
in a cube of chalk

calling the shots
in a blue residue

of precision, sinking
the sunny-side nine ball

running the table
their place of operation—

blood money exchanged
on the fly—

the King's English
held for ransom

a dying language here
like Latin;

like "Nicky the Rack"
who ran into a knife:

"Joe Switch" presiding.
Where worlds collided

in stripes and solids
assorted survival:

cops and robbers
black and blue collars;

the long shot combination
of a hustler and a poet.

Mist Often To Avoid Jetlag

(Read on the side of a spray bottle
in an airplane restroom in First Class)

Mist often to avoid jetlag
Mist often to avoid…
sorrow.
Mist often to avoid the loss of love.
Mist often to avoid the dry spells
that come from wandering alone
in the dessert.
                    Mist often
to avoid the near occasions of sin;
the temptations that take us unawares.
Mist often if you love Jesus.
Mist often for better luck
better sex; a shot at the woman
who sits across the way.
Mist often in lieu of douching.
Mist often to avoid mistaken notions
Mist often…
fret less.
Mist often to save face;
to avoid the linear lines of thought
that so furrow the brow;
that keep us locked up in tiny rooms.
Mist often to avoid lost keys
and glasses and remotes.
Mist often to avoid missing
the boat; the point.
Mist often to avoid not only jetlag
but the whole goddamn jet itself
crashing down.
Mist often in memory of those who fell to earth;
the high horses that have toppled.
Mist often for world peace.
Mist often for a piece of the world.
Mist often you miserable
unworthy slug
then go back to your seat and stay there
for the rest of the flight
until the plane has come
to a complete stop.

LAX

When the flight is over
       the six hours up

the quirky quilt
       of land traversed

East to West—
       a crayon tracing

the parabola
       of the sun—

First Class and Coach
       are enjoined as one.

Headless horsemen
       at a horseless carrousel

stand awaiting the outcome;
       a death by infinity.

A place where baggage mingle
       and name tags dangle

from leather handles
       and big toes.

Squirrels: A Sequel

It's not as if I hadn't written
a poem about it.

A somewhat puffed up tale
of whimsy— I called it:
Squirrels Making Bad Decisions.
It got a few laughs just a week ago—
a horseshoe audience;
a bookstore crowd.

Left unsaid of course:

how we too try to cross
too many roads
in heavy traffic.

How we go about our days
in fits and starts

fall in love to serve up our hearts
on a platinum platter
to those all wrong
for us and other
living matter—

major in that which is mostly minor
minor in that most profoundly major;

buy a used car
from a snake wearing snake-oil
        cologne.
Which raises a question of some import:

on the used car lot of life
what is my Blue Book value?

But back to life on the road—
and from the corner of my eye
I see past my front wheels
and before the back end to follow—

a blur of desperate fur.
                    The heart leaps up

flies off my sleeve
and through the sun-roof glass
followed closely by the mind
now caught up in the steel trap of irony:

Poet turned Perpetrator.

Have a look. Right there.
In the rear view mirror.
Sudden death.
Between the lines.
And to a place beyond
squirrels making bad decisions

to a man unable to brake or swerve
and with nothing left to do

but drive on.

There are elves
within ourselves.

II. S●rt ●f True C●nfessi●ns

"I'M THE MOST TERRIFIC LIAR you ever saw in your life."

Holden Caufield, *The Catcher In The Rye*

John Garfield

There's a need for the telling;
a need for prayer.
I once slept with a woman who slept
with John Garfield. There.
I've told. And in her telling
as I well remember
over red wine, a home cooked
meal and some smoke
as we toyed with platonic chains
about to be broken—
she was a young aspiring dancer;
she was his lover.
One of so very many it seems—
dancers and lovers—
she knew him six months
before he died. Time tells
what legends live.
His star on the Walk of Fame
grows dimmer each day.
He's no Bogart. Though I root for him
(and is that not a form of prayer?)
to have retrospectives
in respected venues;
to be rediscovered
by new generations.

Girl In The Window Seat

Alice Liddell
in cut-off jeans,
tanned and coming back

to L.A.
sits next to
a man in a suit on a plane.

The Math Professor
the Oxford Don
the son of a Deacon father it seems

had just seen her off, after
a reunion that could have been
a disaster— "no picnic" she says.

Pink and pouty— think a small face
that could launch say…
five hundred ships.

Think them falling down
a hole beneath a tree
in Mother Earth.

She calls the Flight
Attendant: "Miss?
Do you have any

crayons?"
"Here," I utter,
"take my pen."

Sort Of True Confessions

How long ago it was, "x 4,"
when Catholic girls kept their chastity intact.
They would lock their door
and banish the key
to a perch out of reach somewhere north
        of Sweden.
Thus roving hands would work up top
like Hannibal crossing a budding Alps.

This being back in the time of voices
deepening and body parts
sprouting hair. This being back
in the time of the longest distance between two points—
church and fate—
a line that ended up behind the curtains.

There we sinners would bow our heads
before the beveled amber glass;
a translucent priest in contemplation.
Call it a springtime of secular seasons
caught in a calendar of pious unreason.
O the guilt, the cleansing, the recycling of sin;
only now do I know what all the groping was for.

In the darkness back then
we would beg for forgiveness.
I've since gone to the lighthouse when the weather was fair—
with apologies to Virginia Woolf—
and have done my penance of three "Hail Mary's"
and given up sweet things for Lent.

Hockey Game

They scored and scored and scored and scored
up and down the ice at will—
I sat there with my date.
First period; first date.

"This doesn't usually happen," I said,
"the puck finding so much net.
Gotta be a record."
She smiled at me. And it was:

Most scoring in the shortest time
between two teams at the start of the game.
Rangers and the Rockies—
before they were "Devils"—

you can look it up.
The rhythm of the contest settled down.
Then rolled over,
exhausted with itself.

And over a cigarette later—
tied at "4" and with still a period to come
she asked me if I'd like to go.

And leaving the game behind
I went.

Chronocide

The killing of time
is there a word for that?

May I suggest
chronocide?

So I sat there committing
chronocide and wondered:

can you do time
for killing it?

Then do more time
for the time spent

doing nothing but
waiting, counting

the days till release?
And if so could there ever be

a chance for parole?
Animals murder it.

And re–murder it.
Then play with it

for good measure.
The cat takes pleasure

in 21 hours of sleep a day.
Then walks away.

Free as the bird
he has swallowed in his dreams.

Klondike

Maybe it's the sea of cards
and the waves rolling in—
wave after wave;
wave after wave—
precise in rhythm
yet random in caliber
that keeps me mesmerized.
Despite my guiding hand
I cannot stop this play of forces.
The cards upon washing ashore
go about their task
defined in ladders
of red-on-black; black-on-red
in the laying of steps in descending order.
Praise for this race
of integrated peoples
extending themselves
for the common good.
Perhaps it is that which keeps me fast
and not the continuum of waves.
I even hold my breath
at the upturn of each new face
from beneath the six
of the seven hills that mark the landscape.
What will it contribute
to this world that it finds?
And yet for their part
the cards bide their time.
Their kingdom, they know
lies above the line
on packs of clouds
where angels gather;
the souls of generations reunited.
I aim to see it come to pass.
And look for kings in any suit
to fill the voids.

Bright Sunshine Brings Falling Ice

photo caption; *The New York Times;* March 8, 2001

Thawing ice fell
from cables
    from five
suspension bridges in New York City;
the veins through which the lifeblood flows.
This in turn forced lanes to close;
stuffing traffic through long-necked bottles—
driving pegs through unyielding holes—
causing ungodly Godot-like delays.
The Bridge and Tunnel Authority
did their best to hack away
at the great forks of ice thrust into
this red apple day.
Their goal, to remove, the remaining Swords
of Damocles that hung above
the crawl of captive cars.
No telling what time one would get home.
I myself walked in the door at nine
    but knowing
that the first full step of any twelve-step journey
starts with a thawing out;
    the cold turkey thanksgivings
for being at least on the right road at last.
The wakeup call;
    the epiphanies,
that first new day when the sun appears
to burn a hole in the fog
    leaving revealed
the skyscrapers born of The Great Depression
pointedly looming high above your head.

Coffee House: An Encounter   Of A Kind

Tattoo   torn T-shirt   not my type
she sits there   poring   over
a chessboard   pieces   a book:
"Chess: The Fundamentals   For Beginners."

Sipping   some sort   of house concoction
through the slot   in the lid   by rote
she is   all business.   The Second Coming
of Kasparov   hidden behind   cool shades
the sun   screaming hot   like a maniac through
the plate glass   window   bent on blinding
anyone   in   its way.
I   from the flip side   come in
"on little cat feet"   on a hunch   hat in hand
to offer   a game   a chance
to practice   a real life   situation.

"No.   Sorry.   Just
waiting.   Myself.   Playing."
Accent?   Eastern   European?
Accent?   Middle   Eastern?
Friend?   Foe?   *Pas*?
I retreat   to thumb through   a Newsweek
to check   who's up   or down
to see   whose side   we're on
to get what   this week   matters.
Apparently   upon   a reconsideration
she's there   at my side: "Please to play?"

She's white.   I'm Black.   Knight to "f3"
"e4"   the much preferred: "center squares first"
but in this   her style   the game begins
and she moves   every   which way
off book   off strategy   grinding tactics
bad squares   abandoned squares   a bishop
blocking   the king's pawn   the queen's entrance
postponing   castling   chances
traps   tricks   poisoned pawns
the knight fork   Christ   like I won't see it coming?

I don't.   I'm down.   A piece
left hanging   out there   like boxer shorts
a yellow   polka-   dotted
banana   blunder.   She smiles.
I tingle.   I've been: dumbed down
done in   thrown down   the dumbwaiter.
Damn.   Next   my knight
gets pinned.   Then the rooks   hemmed in
the back row   a mess   much
mass   hysteria   setting in.

She toys with me   beneath   the table
apologizing   for errant   knees.
Then her hand   comes up   to clutch
her Lady   Macbeth   of a Queen
her tattoo   of thorns   dripping
blood   muscle   bound
taunt   and tightening   within the squeeze
a master's thesis   in "The Art   of Strangulation"
she looks   to go in   for the kill
red hair   on fire   smoking sunlight
frames   her face   casting downward
angled   almost   hiding
the smirk   behind   her naked
ambition: to nail down   g5. Done!

Her majesty   stands there crowing   as if a cock.
It's all over   save for   the dying.

Ah but   wait but   see but
hold   but   just a sec
seems like   suggesting just   maybe a bit
premature   this thrust of hers?   I parry.

Game   Turning   Point.

Bitch.   In a blur   I let fly
the pieces   pounding anvil   of the heart
wet palms   the scent of   perfumed sweat
changing worlds   the creaking   of chairs
the up-   ending   of seats
finger tips   going off   to join temples
bottom lips   being licked   and bit
then broken   skin   peeling
I now up   The Piece   and trading down:
the Endgame   dear   is near.
The math of it   like water   seeps in
to seek   its own level   a shift in the ocean
to bring   the finite to   the infinite.
A matter of   time   and space
meted out   in squares   made easy
for schoolboy   counting.   Sensing this
then reading it   in the realm   of remainder forces
her smattering   of pawns   little choices
bald men   wandering   lost in the dessert
the Bad Bishop   still bogging them   down

her dark glasses   come off   her face undone
the cheekbones down   from off   their high horses
lips   as tight   as Ebeneezer's purse
elves working   to preempt   a pout
eyes seen   for the first time   seem
too small   too close   near crying.

She extends   a hand   in limp resignation
I   her grandmaster now   standing up
kiss her   full   on the mouth
finding   with my tongue   a pearl.

41

jesters

we are all amusing ourselves out here
cracking each other up

taking meetings
meeting meddlers
peddling with peddlers

we are building buildings
and building better

mousetraps while making
low fat cheese

near which the mice
will not go near

we are
the conjurers up of
gods and saints
we are the lead
in the stained glass windows

granted there's gravity
no laughing matter

the yin and yang of planets beyond
the scope of our telescopes

but all the rest
is swimmingly up for grabs

and grab we must
at brass rings and straws

(not necessarily in that order)

as we try to tiptoe across the wire
holding on to our balance poles
working the world without Annette

(and God do we miss her)

on our unicycles
we are flywheels in the ointment
rolling through
the nitty-gritty

keepers keeping
all the balls in the air

The Poet's Lot: A Wife

My wife comes into the room as I work
to tell me about the virgin moon.

How it hides behind a veil of clouds
and peeks demurely through the branches

at the window behind me;
the one that faces the side of the hill.

The one that appears to be on fire
in the alpenglow of an August sunset.

It's all there. Night and day
at a point of resolution.

I could see it for myself, she tells me, if only
I would turn around before it passes.

Go away. Can't you see
I'm trying to write poems?

Lot's Wife: A Poet

Nameless one
so unafraid

to turn to look
not only in the eye of beauty
but in the fall from grace as well.

Owed To A Cab

I stepped out into the night to hail a cab.
"O hail great Yellowed Checkered Whale."
Take me home upon your back

tied down like Ahab
on last legs beckoning
throughout the ocean of streets

shellacked with rain.
O weave your magic
through the conundrums of traffic

and the twisted brethren–
their brains afire–
staggering out of Nightclub Hell.

How many times have you saved my soul?
Whisked me away from my trysts of folly
my wayward obsessions and bacchanal feasts,

the days of beauty; the nights of the beast?
You who have kept sacred for me always
the glow of your "Taxi" top burning.

III. The Lamplight Glowing

"You always have a green light that burns all night
at the end of your dock."

Jay Gatsby, *The Great Gatsby*

Stale Mates

Unwittingly, the white
pawn blocks the path of
the anxious black queen
hell-bent on checkmate—
the sound of the ticking
clock a deafening roar
threatening to devour
her in one swallow.

                    Curse the gods that
                    have fixed this lowly
                    centurion at this point
                    in time and space wreaking
                    havoc on the universe,
                    casting a shadow on the
                    orbit of Cassandra spinning
                    in and out of control.

Were not the moves
fated to flow from a
grand design, a churning
kaleidoscope of shards
of glass, but all the
same, a sequence of
squares each lighting
the way to another?

                    Patterns of black and white
                    defining the boundaries of
                    not only what was possible,
                    but what was probable— at
                    worst a draw by mutual consent.
                    And now an endgame that no
                    one wants, compelled to be
                    played on without resolution.

The Fledgling

Sometimes I would come by morning light;
we worked the off-hours and then if at all.
Like an innkeeper's wife in the crack at the door
you would peer through with crow's feet eyes
　　　slowly working
the latch to let me in. Then part your robe—

let it slide down supple shoulders and fall
to the hardwood floor. Holder. The beheld.
We took our turns as might the winds
　　　caught
in a conflict of seasons; androgynous storms
set upon the sky of your bed.

And always new magic to be found. The finger tips pressing
the bulb that would blossom surprising us both
with its delicate power; a delirium drawn
from the suckled breast; the alchemy
of scent and smoke and rivulets of sweat.

A woods of mystery so dense its truth,
could be probed only just so far then abandoned;
a labyrinth of menace and stalking grace.
Hunter and prey; the overtaking—
the becoming overcome. All this—

compliments of a wakeup call. Some mornings
I now lie thinking of your crow's feet eyes
so blind to the random flights of the fledgling
to whom the world, but a golden worm
to be swallowed along with the best of intentions.

Paulie's

When Coke came in green glass bottles
    and we
the miniature gamblers and horse traders
were gathering at the corner candy store—
baseball cards, the currency—

you were somewhere off being born,
setting in motion an odd set of gears.

Later, beneath a ceiling of squares
    in rococo tin
that held the stone clouds of *Lucky Strikes*
and dangled the bare bulb of moon above
a graduated game of cards—
The Back Room

where we mannequins sat deciphering our hands.

So nothing stood between you and I
    dear Beatrice.

Nothing but card games
front of store and back;

flipping and trading
of gods and demigods;

while waiting to fill
an inside straight.

March 4, 1881

When men of mien wore muttonchops
and you were the belle of the inaugural ball
James A. Garfield flirted with you.
The twentieth President of the United States
said how a lucky a young man I was as he swept you
clear across the floor. The minions parted.

Your goldenrod gown was a whirl of taffeta,
as the eyes of the nation and spouses were upon you.
Lucretia, in her gown, of lavender lace
that in time would fade to an oyster white—
now on display at the Smithsonian as I speak—
smiled, fulfilling, the vow of First Ladies.

And I played my good-natured card to her ace.
I remember the applause when your grand waltz was over.
And how later in the backroom over a snifter of brandy
and the good coarse smoke of fresh-cut cigars
the theme was reprised of your beauty... my lucky stars.
His assassination soon after would wound you forever.

Hotel: Right Bank

Window wide open
       casements drawn in

to their fullest extent
       no screen between

man and the elements
       man and his woman.

No, nothing to stifle
       this impromptu floor show

of lightning and thunder;
       the spiked heels of rain

tap dancing on rooftops
       and street cobblestone.

No, nothing to derail
       any passion train.

And still with no sign
       of an oncoming breeze

it stays preternaturally
       dry inside

with nary a ripple
       in the sheets.

Amniocentesis

She is walking around somewhere
carrying my youth.

And I float with her every step in the fluid
of past tense. It drips away.
And I grow smaller.

Conceived that summer on the whim of the ride—
a streak of steel through the underground brain—
we would fly off at tangents at every stop:

a dip in Bethesda Fountain
where nudity reveled in its imperfection;

concerts heavy with smoke and jungle;

serpentine tongues forever in search
of the spot or a taste of life's apple.

The sign at the Central Park Zoo might have read:
Please Don't Feed The Nihilists.

Call it sport, after all
this was all before Cable.
But now each year

the baby shrivels in her belly.
Gestation put through a time machine.

Ode To A Starbucks Girl

Our Lady of the Latte— one
So brightly beautiful; so beautifully bright
And naked as the day she walked out from the sea—
Returns as if compelled by the sound
Of her own sweet song.

Then propelled by the fingers
Of memory— memory
As old as the first drop of water—
She swims in a silent frenzy
As the night beats on its drum.

Beneath the stars and above the starfish—
Each splayed in its five points—
The sizzling brine swirls about her sea legs
Shaped by Neptune's lathe and iridescent
Deigned to be split on the point of dawn—

The scent of the sea as she lay beached—
Inviting every man ever lost at sea.
And it must have worked for they couldn't stop coming.
The day's catch caught in a network complete
With eels and the one odd shoe.

And once left dry they never left.
Never returned to the home-cooking kitchens
Nor the Queen Bee women—
They called their wives—
Awaiting to pick their sorry flesh.

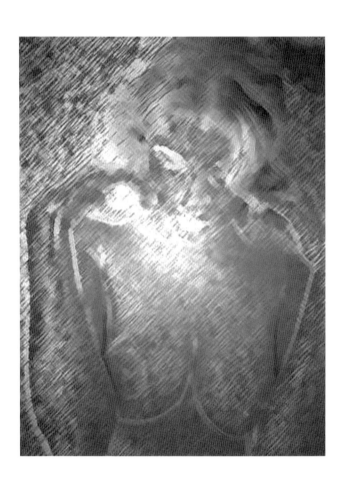

Beverly Boulevard

Old World Money
rolling down the street—
you can tell by the backs of their cars. And then

by their macadamian heads transfixed
in the sunset of the wheel.

Of course the widows-in-waiting sit
beside them
winnowing out stations
to catch a snatch of news
while pointing out a signpost up ahead.

The path of the car—
a mad staggers of doubt,
works the road as a raindrop might
a windshield—
                        If

you ever see me driving down
a boulevard this way
please take me out and shoot me— "MOVE,
you old bastard!
Get off the godforsaken road!"

Shoot me you hear
if I ever— I mean ever
so much as drift
over one yellow line
with my nut head slowly turning
to ask you for directions or

maybe

to tell you

how wonderful

the ride has been.

My love.

One Red Rose

1.

The words of love it seems have been used up.
The sweet and bittersweet ones;
the ones so trite and true;
the ones long spoken and sung
in all forms of verse and rhyme.

Shall I compare thee to a summer's day?
Or count the ways how *I love thee?*

Shall I sing that
Love is a many splendored thing?
That *you light up my life?*
Or toy with a rendition of *In The Still Of The Night?*
Note how *you walk in beauty like the night?*

Or *the way you wear your hat?*
Sip your tea? Call you Sue?
And exclaim at the top of my precious lungs
how *she sure knows what to do?*

Or call you Daisy and cry out to the world
how *she almost drives me crazy?*
Or how: *You always have a green light that burns all night*
at the end of your dock.

2.

It wasn't to be this way. I was to be
the man with a mission
whose cup would runneth over
and spill across state lines;
no longer in need of words of this kind.
The quest? To even up the score.
O how I hated the death of love so.
And so to death,
the words that describe it as well.

And then one day you walked in my door
shamelessly carrying
one red rose.

One that opened up my eyes
and then its own petals.
Lush and velvety
a dark mouth in burgundy,
it swallowed up the world I knew.
And echoed every love word ever uttered.
And the universe teetered and tottered.

Then hell froze over.
And the devil went skating.
And the angels went dancing
on the head of a pin.
And Dean Martin stood off in a corner crooning
a love song holding
that very rose.

Tin
(A Tenth)

The years we live as one,
like hummingbirds, fly too
quickly. I give the lamp three
rubs— the wishing game: for
that we may sail as mates, five
decades and more. (At ninety-six
I can soft-shoe away). That seven
times weekly let us ruminate
on those moments, so benign;
the dreams so soon forgotten.

Symmetries

One circle of trees
one ring of fire

a song of earth and
candle power.

Enjoined? A dance.
A tango of flame.

IV. Just Business

"You shouldn't let that broken jaw influence you...
it was business, not personal."

Tom Hagen, *The Godfather*

"Tell Mike it was only business, I always liked him."

Salvatore Tessio, *The Godfather*

Miss

So on a trip back from way
the hell across the country—
a new business presentation—

the wine
is so fine.

At such times kicking back
with the plane at rest
on an eider down of air

and the warm nuts they serve so tasty—
pecans, pistachios
a cashew here or there—
I think the thought:

these are the moments
that I will miss most. *Miss?*

Can I have another glass of Chardonnay?

The common stock like a stork is flying.
Yet it's the "stand-up" routines
in wood-paneled places
making the cases
for mass communications:

      O the power of positioning the message;
      the lines that make the heart beat faster—

this too I will miss. *Oh, Miss?*

Can I please have a pillow upon which to rest
my oh so strategic head?
And this time make it a "red."

We told them that we
are about building Brand Leaders
around the world.

I will miss this boasting and busting of buttons.

Not to mention the sparks that spill across the table;
the spumes off the top of topless heads—
clueless but convinced;
unknowing but convincing.

We do not know what it is you do
but we'll tell the world how well you do it:
TV, the Internet, Outdoor, Print.

And not a word will be lost
in the linguistic linguini
that marks most translations.

After all, we have offices
in every Godforsaken country.
Even Viet Nam. *'scuse me.*

Miss?

Blue Sky Session At Morning

Dabbling in creation, a process
of thinking out loud
magic markers running wild
(In the beginning there was light…)
across the big pads mounted on easels—
big as the skies of Butte, Montana—
the better to catch the windstorms blowing
    east to west

and all to market a car
the world has been waiting for.

What kind of world is that exactly?
And what do I wish to be while in it?
The one who sits idling in some vehicle
    of another's dream
or the one who steps out to explore?

Imagine Columbus and his presentation
on overhead slides with computations:

Your majesty as you can see
the world is round instead of flat;
defying the wisdom of our day.
And therefore what goes around
must come around…

I'll need three ships; two thousand men.

"We could do some sort of promotion"
says someone goosing me out of my stupor.
"Come in for a test drive today and get
frequent flyer miles and a pen.
One that writes upside down
like the astronauts use."

One with which to write our epitaphs
as we lay dying?
Or to write on the Sistine Chapel ceiling?
Or perhaps on the soles of dangling feet?

Or better yet
let's do something really cool:
like sell ice to the Eskimos on the internet.
E-mail every igloo.
Follow up with a CD ROM.
ROM wasn't built in a day, gets jotted down
on a blue-lined yellow legal pad.
Possible tag line for the next great campaign?

Got milk? Got milk? Got milk?

Why don't we do T-shirts. Pass them out
in the malls of America:

> LOOK AT ME.
> I'M MORE THAN THIS.
> TAKE ME OUT FOR A TEST DRIVE.
> NEVER BRING ME BACK.

Down Quarter

On coming back home
after having been summoned
up north once again
to tell our tale

we men of business are mulling matters
(in open shirt fashion now
with the passing of ties).

We do a *pas de deux* about the net
of gain and loss
demand   supply

the sales trends trembling—
but along whose fault line?

Rejection rides shotgun in the window seat;
failure, its feet, in the aisle.
Me? I play with my swizzle stick
crammed somewhere in between them

and wonder whatever happened
to Ellen O' Gorman:

blue eyes   freckles   golden hair.

Morning On The Elevator

That she could step on to this
Otis elevator every day
Looking for all the world
Like that Cosmo Girl:
The daughter Hemera
Born of Night and Darkness.
Working her hair with manicured hand
A mane of golden sun
Thrusting forth
Her bounty of cleavage:
She of Accounts Receivable
Eternal Spring.
He of Accounts Payable
In short-sleeved white shirt
A couple of pens
Clung to the breast pocket
Windsor knot in a tie falling
Far short of the bay window
Begins with still another
Big hello. The small talk ensues.
The references to this world
Of names and respective departments.
Like this new guy Klein in Arrears
A transfer from New York
The home office
Who's hard to work with.
Or Mickelson in Marketing.
Or Laurie's leaving Legal. But to hell with them
And their scheme of things.
He wants to tell her
He loves her.
Right here.
Wants more than that.
Wants to press himself
Hard up against her.
Like in the movies
When all pretense of what the chance meeting
Is all about falls away.

The moment laid bare.
Ripe for the taking.
And he wants to run his hands
Wildly through her hair
Like lions on the Serenghetti.
And encircle her 24 inch waist—
Taste her mouth.
Smear her lipstick.
Take her right there.
On the elevator;
Beg her to run away with him
While parting her thighs like the Red Sea.
That he step lively
Much less run anywhere
With all the wheezing. Cigarettes. He should quit.
The doctor told him so— but what the hell.
Aren't we all living
On you know what time anyway.
And cut out red meat? What for?
Fish and rabbit food?
An extra lean year or two?
But at least if in lieu of small talk, if only
That a hothouse plant
Of revelations might grow between them.
Like who is she doing it with these days?
And how she likes to do it?
And what she thinks about blowjobs.
And that thing with the cigar—
Right there in the Oval Office?
He might show her a thing or two
If he had the chance. Fat chance,
And he catches the pun in his moon of a head
Spinning weightless in silent laughter
Mingling with all manner of words unspoken.
He catches his reflection
on the back of the closing doors:
The Fat Guy Sweating.
She gets off at her floor.

Executive Travel: A Sonnet

- Oh, these short hops in and out of hotels;
- The body barely dents the sheets
- In the clashing time zones, the ride on the coattails
- Of the corporation; the fight for sleep.
- Arising before seven, they'll be clients to meet:
- General Matters and their management teams.
- In marathon sessions, through snow, rain or sleet.
- Angel ideas fight the imps of dreams:

    o Of flight connections and departure schemes
    o To circumvent distempered climates.
    o Of the car chauffeurs who will hold up our names
    o To which we'll respond like well-trained primates.

        - These keepers who will take us to some skyscraper phallus;
        - Arrivals, departures— the search for the chalice.

On The Avenue Of The Americas

They slice off the excess fat of encounter
with butcher-knife scowls
                                    then cut corners— poof!

They disappear.
Down they go, down
the rapid transit holes
or up into shoebox buildings
set on end. I want to follow
in their wake and shout: RELAX.

You see… it's been done.

The great god Churn
spits in the ocean.
Then wave after wave
year after year
the broomsticks come marching
unrelenting
toting like water buckets
their black bags of business.
Waltz with me scalawags
beneath a sky of delicious gray.

Jaywalk, cab-dodge
camouflaged in your trench coats—
that never seem to go out of season—
across the penciled grids
of the Great White Way.

Movement makes the place hum mantras on moving—
fast, faster, fastest—
on making more moves.

But have we considered
dancing in the wheel?
Buck-and-Winging it through the maze?

Someone once issued a decree—
                                        left town
and ever since St. Alban it's all been
heavy heels and hissy buses,
sordid subterranean trains;
a yellow smear of taxi—
everywhere; limo lizards—
up and down the elevators
4/4's time on escalators,
hippo ferries hugging harbor
skateboards, 10-speeds,
arriving planes.

The gargoyles hacking fire from their perches set in stone
can't scare them away.
In fact up there is where
the pigeons come home to roost
come dark.

Corporate Colors

Here I sit
holed up in
a corner office
fortressed by
a huge rectangular slab of granite.

Apologia to Magritte:
Cici n'est pas une bureau
but an expression of
"a desk."
A bequest in deference to tenure
    abandoned by
some hotshot;
a "creative guy."
He was going to set the place on fire
but was gone rather quickly
with nary a spark
nor cinder of shame.

I take stabs at trying to scratch out of
The Box.
An escape inspired
not by the legacy of

"The Desk"

but by a need to fill a blank sheet
    of snow white paper
with scads of color
to cause someone like
a mother or Sister
of St. John the Baptist
to bend down and take
some small notice. Call it:

The Secret Life Of A Man Of Business.

A "numbers cruncher" given to
the recklessness of designer ties
and subversive coloring
behind closed doors—
SUDDENLY A KNOCKING.

Insolent interlopers,
    don't they know
        it's time for "chow"?
            or I might be "dealing"?
                "six-figures" or more?
                    on the "squawk box"?
                        with some "honcho"?
                            from the "Big Apple"?
                                fix the "bottom line"?

Pinter Pause.
Santa Claus?

Or maybe
I've been found out.
Someone from... who knows?
Scotland Yard? *Please come along.*

But they will never get me
no matter how tight,
how golden the handcuffs—
truth be known
I'm about *thisclose,*
to replacing all
the "corporate-logoed" pens
with a box of Crayolas—
all 64 in perfect array;
eight New Age colors
joining the fray.
Which raises the question:

why the mourning the death of Raw Umber?
It is quite apparent
the world wants Fuchsia.
And there will be
no turning back.

Haiku... And Counting

The ant works harder
than seventeen syllables
winter, spring, summer

fall.

On A Smoking Break

Outlaws now
        they cluster in the bowels
           of the building on white
      plastic chairs
    set like teeth.
They sit inhaling with lament.
They sit
   each exhale in contempt.
     The world has turned on them
        as worlds have been known to do.
              The ashtray at center,
       a pit of burnt offerings;
     homage to the devil.
The ashtray at center
    a gesture of kindness
      and corporate loathing: "If you must
        steal company time, we ask
          you keep it clean
            this scene
        of your crime."
They mumble in monotones
   this ill-suited lot;
      shadows passing
        in the same hell believing
    there's been some mistake
  but they play along.
And hatch brain-dead plans to break out.
  Yet with nothing afoot
    they pass the time
      conjuring ribbons
        of blue-gray genies
      and spirits and ghosts
    that swirl in a silent
    tangle of death.
Thus the haze holds firm between us:
  the redefined living
   and the tribal dead.
      Come upstairs
       to the conference table
         cut from the heart
      of the redwood tree.
    There we might trace the rings
        of our consanguinity.

V. They

"Who's they? Who, specifically,
  do you think is trying to murder you?"

"Every one of them."

"Every one of whom?"

"Every one of whom do you think?"

"I haven't any idea."

"Then how do you know they aren't?"

Clevenger and Yossarian, *Catch 22*

A Death In The Family

When God died
I couldn't get the day off
from work
            we were busy.

I sent my condolences.
Though I hardly knew him
the truth be told.

Flowers seemed beside the point. Besides,

surely Catholicism would cover
all floral arrangements:
those thorny wreaths of theology
to hang on every cathedral door.

The Jews would send sweets.
        Sit shiva.

Set up college trust funds
in His name.
                "His" here being
the operative Word:
the quote/unquote.

Conspiracy theories
would emerge and abound.
        After all,
He seemed so... well,
invincible.

A "Mafia hit"
some had suggested.
An Italian-American,
I took offense.
And pointed at the atheist
who played chess every day in the park.

And the Jews already bristling
about the "Christ thing"—
That Accusation—
made certain in the press, that
"Never Again."

Meanwhile the WASPs
would go about their business,
as buzzing bees about their honey;
the mix of old
and new world money—
a stiff upper lip
and all that jazz.

In New Orleans, they sang the blues.

All other belief systems need not apply.

A conundrum for
the Buddhist watchers;
the New Age left out in the snow.

Places of worship
flew the flags of state
half-mast.
                    Half-assed
editorials,
suggested maybe,
we had *all* pulled the trigger.
Though no gun,
smoking or otherwise,
was ever found.

The Fordham Baldies

The nuns would whoosh about in black and white
     the incense churning
in the parish church
fanned in their wake
         their clickers clicking

to cue us to sit,
to stand, to kneel,

to beg God for His tender mercy.

But neither prayer nor the desk in which
we carved the names
of Dick & Jane

under which we would hide from The Atom Bomb—
in omnia paratus—
would save us

for when *The Fordham Baldies* might come.

These "baldies" were "baddies"
         they had razor blades
in the tips of their shoes,
or so we heard tell:
"the better to kick your faggot ass."

And how they would take
the "A" train from The Bronx
to swoop down upon grade schools
sneering
     their bald pates— brass doorknobs—
brightly shining
       taking no prisoners;

baptisms under
the fiercest of fires.
We might all wind up like St. Stephen
the first martyr.

Monday? Tuesday? Or maybe just when
we'd forget to be looking
and leave our guardian angels down:

"New York, New York—
a helluva town."

Meanwhile the Penguins and their Mother Superior
made life on the ice floe
                    a pilgrimage to heaven

worked in increments of inches
with a judgment day to come.

Though *The Fordham Baldies* themselves never came.
At least as far
as anyone can recall.

The Guards Of Art

The young men and women
of various ethnicities
stand guard here protecting
priceless paintings;
white guy paintings.

Dead white guy painters
who dripped on the floor;
who cut off their ears;
dealt in soup cans
                    painted the flag
in blasphemous colors;
painted pipes and claimed they weren't;

who drew melting clocks
and two-sided faces
of three or more eyes
    or who otherwise
took to tagging
the sides of the passing scene.

These guards are all that stand between:
Man With Razor
Or *Can Of Spray*
and a stilled life;
one with no apples or pears.
These strokes of genius on canvas
that hold us together;
the things we stare at
but can't quite see;
that something that would cut to the bone if defiled.

Do they who stand guard
ever look at it his way?
Or just at the paintings?
Or neither of these—
                    rather simply keeping tabs
to see that we keep our curious fingers
to ourselves.

Egg Life

Curl up inside of an (egg) and hear
the murmurs of your heart while in there
dismissing those of unknown sources
seeping through the brittle shell.

Stay in/come out whoever you are.
Either nothing matters
or everything does. Meanwhile

                        cracks are to be feared.
Once started, they tend to traverse opaquely
in stunning elliptical patterns
top to bottom and back again.
Then the offhand blow…
they find you out.

With no say in it, you'll learn
to speak the Mother Tongue.
                        In time
you'll learn to sign on dotted lines.

In time you'll acquire
keys to admire
on your golden chain.

Which of course they will pull
with some regularity;

which of course will change the shape
of things to become.

The Ventriloquist

You don't seem to see the ventriloquist anymore.
One man made "in the image of God"
holding his own facsimile— albeit downsized in wood.
The former decked out in formal attire;

the latter— the knees, at ninety degrees
bent beneath a pair of snazzy slacks.
And perfectly at home with a hand up his back;
head in constant spin as if to keep tabs on the master.

Then the eye rolls telegraphing it cannot believe
the drivel coming from this crazy man's mouth.
The audience— it's own mouth agape— devours it whole.
An art form in perversity— this talking to oneself?

And through lips locked in semi-smile no less?
And through teeth enmeshed and gritted?
Yet he would swear, that the dummy has a life of its own
if someone were so inclined as to inquire.

How did it start? How did it end?
What first impulse conceived this creation:
a frontispiece in wood for cracking wise?
And how long did it go on to rapt attention;

this repartee between, the mahogany and the flesh?
Was it we then who decided that we all had heard enough?
Or had the master sensed his time had come
to move his lips and move on.

Game Show Host

What is there to be said for this telegenic creature
with his checkered threads and caviar eyes?
And sweeping gestures, measured so,
downstage where unfolds the draperies:
    revealing more than the mind can swallow
    prompting a rubberneck response so shallow?

With chair and cracking quip he eggs on
the ample housewives, their bouncing breasts,
as they gather steam in panting pursuit
of service-for-eight and a luggage set.
    This mercury-haired fox leers at their girth
    through fine cut slits in a sandalwood mirth.

The Grand Presider, the devilish divider,
meting out each precious prize
with watered-down kisses that flush the terrain
of these moon-faced women— our mothers and wives.
    A withered heart behind his lapel,
    pumps and pimps in this atrophied cell.

Yes, do play us as we wish to be played. And tingle
our spines with knowing fingers. Quiver
our strings in the bonus round— we are yours.
At least till the credits roll by— every sliver.
    Though the credit be ours, you were born on our watch;
    make it up to us please, with your seamless dispatch.

BOBBY HOGUE

'52 Cards

They peer out from under
the shelter of their caps—
winter eyes in a summer game.
The mark of the journey—

from the toil of the fathers
to the triumph of the sons—
clings to their jerseys
like Lenten ashes.

The countenance in these tinted portraits—
that of military men on eve of battle—
speaks directly to we who will listen;
to we who remember

the Homer Kings and Icarian phenoms.
They who burned and crashed
on the wicked path
of the devil curve ball.

But who exactly is Bobby Hogue?
Handsome gent; must have done fine
with the ladies and their mind.
Then left no sign. Save

for the cardboard visage
evading our eyes.
He knows we have seen his underside
in the attic of American lore;

those summers before
the colors began to bleed across
the Paul Revere Yankee cloth.
The little boys

on a sailor's night
catching fireflies
just off
the white front porch.

Collars

Of Phillips heads and molly bolts
    they speak;

their names in red script, sewn
above the breast pocket—
true blue work shirts:
Mike... and Larry... and Pete.

There are no poets named Pete.

Where do they come from?
these men who weave
these tangled webs—
networks of wire
    not to deceive,
but for all the inbred reasons;
like Sammy Spider
plying the family trade.

They leave the tables—
    actuary and otherwise—
the probabilities on which way
the numbers will go
to us:

guys who tend to eschew the name Gus.

They ogle the chicks going by;
    the politics, Apple Pie,
incorrectly worn on their short sleeves;
    tattoos of daggers and snakes peeking out—
"ahead of the curve"—

I never knew a longshoreman named Merv.

And I wonder what a plumber is like in bed?
Whether he knows how to plumb for the G-Spot?

We are all, after all, men
        under the skin—
theirs only more so.

Like bark. Roughhewn, scarred,
from laying all that pipe and weaving wire
into the neurobiotics
of our daily lives.
                Zeus himself

shrivels before the thunderbolts
of a licensed electrician.
They who would walk through dry walls to tell us
it's all fixed— we can go about our business:

the pounding of books,
in a world dark with knowledge.

Nine men stand waiting
under storm clouds that gather.
Someone asks for time.

●

Off The Bat Of Berra

It ain't overt
till it's overt.
Then it's over.

●

The Third World War

In the beginning
there was the end:

The Colossus of Rhodes
had once again been toppled.

Though this time not while protecting the harbor.
We still had the Lady up to that task.

This time the stumps of those muscular legs remained
from the fire fueled by contempt in the form
of crashing planes
                    caught on camera

where no flowers in the fields of mythology can grow
too far off the main road
of concrete, iron, glass and steel;
blood and mangled human form.

This time was in "real time" —
an instant understanding
    of plight and doom

then ensuing good-byes
via cellular phones.

And death came dressed in foreign clothes.

He looked like the man at the falafel stand
near 666 at 5th
                and he did not bother

with the good form of knocking
and other such gestures in dignity.

And so that this time
the whole planet Earth itself was shaken.

It said as much in its cluster of candles
            that encircled its girth
in flickering flame.

Again, all seen live
through the eyes of technology.

And in the end
there was the beginning:

the prodigal sons and daughters returning
from their bell-bottomed days
to their Mother Country
to the Founding Fathers
to Flag and family dog

now dry-nosed and dying
in the corner.

Scientists Bring Light To Full Stop, Hold It, Then Send It On Its Way

Headline: *New York Times*, Thursday, January 18, 2001

They do stuff like this all the time.
      Mostly,
while we are sleeping.

Discover things like
once-upon-a-time water
under the surface of Mars;
new planets and solar systems—
they even midwife the birth of stars.

They clone sheep and cows
and discover DNA

so we'll know that O. J. was there.

They set up the internet one afternoon
while we were still blowing
smoke rings in the face
of the Surgeon General
across a Formica table—

put pilots in the palm
of our unworthy hands
many moon landings later.

Ah, the moon.
A piece of cheesecake for them.

For they felt in their brains they could do it and did.

They even taught a machine to play chess;
it stuck a dagger through Kasparov's heart.

101

They make smart bombs and rubber bullets
and guns that merely stun.
They find black holes in light years
beyond the sun;

the Quark ought to know that there's no place to hide.

And on the Seventh Day
do they rest?

Or is there no day at the beach in the heavens;
no time to build castles
in the clouds?

Greek And Latin Lit: 101

Upon entering the room, you simply said,
in a manner of fact, "Yes it's true. He's dead."
    And proceeded to go on with that Friday's class.

That part where Medea serves up the last
of her children chopped up on a plate
    for Jason, his ravishing appetite to sate.

And unsuspectingly he does.
And we knew just how vile a meal that was
    on this day when the classics were undermined

by Dallas: A Tragedy for Modern Time.
Our time. And you took it away;
    the right to succumb to grief— kept at bay.

You venomous, vainglorious man.
You served up Medea at a moment when
    butchered progeny was the last thing we needed.

With a smirk you watched as we sat defeated.
Was some point proved? Did we pass out test?
    I've wondered why we stayed bound to our desks.

Too civilized, I suppose, to stomp out of the room.
We should have sent you right to your doom;
    trampled underfoot and dragged across campus

as Achilles, passionate warrior he was,
had done with the carcass of Hector.
    And now each time at that vector,

that November day crossing of another year,
I taste the irony in your name, Mr. Lear.
     And can only wish you an afterlife fixed

to a barge floating down the river Styx
winding its way through the sewers of Dallas;
     encircling the sins of fraud and malice.

And each time in the passing, pray you are sprayed
with the brains that flew from that motorcade.
     In response to my whereabouts that day, I tell
     how you taught us, you bastard, the classics so well.

SECOND GUN

THEORIES

While Jack As Ever

I traveled across the country to photograph
surviving men and women of that period.

Richard Avedon

Eyes gone to glass; eyebrows all askew
in odd elfin configurations.
Some try on a smile. Others?
Their faces reassemble
for the clarion's last call.
And it turns on them like rotting fruit.

Where were you, when you heard? The years—
The Grand Inquisitor. The question? Always.
Even when not asked. But the years can only
be blamed for that which makes you
at one with the liver spots.

Some of you, if nothing else,
might have bothered to wear the right tie.
The motorcade, The Calling,
was once of pin-striped precision—
a carrousel from which you seized
the brass ring that was your day.

And it seemed as if it just passed by
reflected in your high glossed hair
heralding the Camelot colors.

Yet all they can muster— these mere pastels
of their once shining selves—
through the bars of this cruel cage of irony
a stare.

While Jack, as ever, the handsome prince.

Plotting Soil

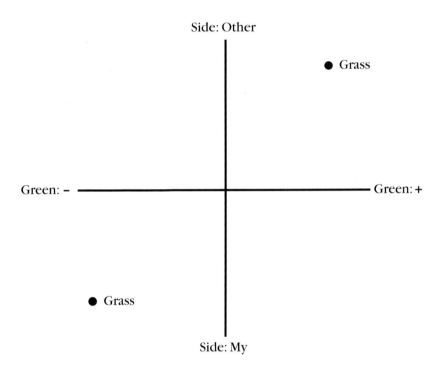

Dóminus Vobíscum

The wind out front stirs
in deference to autumn
and the leaves play tag in celebration
this Thanksgiving Day.

And then as if spun from this whirligig—
someone is at the door.
A repeated knocking dims the house noise
the TV chatter, the can of voices:
surrogates, friends, a relation or two.

Messengers have come with news from God;
their theology hidden behind hemisphere smiles.
And why ask with The Word delivered
right to the door
like *Dómino's Pízza*.

Then they tip their hand and a make a play
        for my soul.
In defense I reach back
for some altar boy Latin, leaning
forward on the open front door:

Introíbo ad altáre Dei—
Ad Deum qui lætíficat
Juventútem meam.

I will go to the altar of God—
The God who gives joy to
My youth.

This liturgical gambit with the bishop door
cuts through their diagonal path of attack—
renders them mute;
sends them away.

Tossing their pamphlet in the trash
    with the gizzards—
that part of the bird that no one wants—
I come to the table
raise a glass of red wine
    a crust of brown bread
        and beseech the assemblage:

Take and eat you all of this;
for this is my body.
Take you all and drink of this
for this is the chalice of my blood...

VI. Scenes

"The world is a stage, but the play is badly cast."

Oscar Wilde, *Lord Arthur Savile's Crime*

Buddies

After oceans of Beaujolais
    we cannot see the shore.
        Stubborn seamen; sea legs gone
            we brace ourselves against the night.
                Distant gemstone lights transfix us
            on this deck though lost at sea,
                the grand design behind their luminescence.

You stayed too long; I served too well.
    The points of rambling discourse catching
        on the ragged jetties of incoherence;
            this and that and nothing really.
                It is time to abstain from the bacchanal feast
                yet loathe to leave, we cling to the table.
                    With hungry hearts, parched minds and bitter tongues

we tease with tattered tales of former lives;
    the salad days of stage; the bygone wives we knew.
        There just as well might be a plank extending past this deck
            upon which we might walk its length together.
                You opt instead for the keys to your car; I—
            like a pillar of salt stand forever
            and watch you drive away.

A Return To Yankee Stadium

The first time I came hurtling through
that ovarian tunnel on the sparks of friction
and the scream of wheels— I clung to breath;
a child to face the head–on crash

of dark into day at the end of the ride.
Below the subway station loomed
a wedge of concrete birthday cake.
With emerald topping and pumpkin filling

and marshmallow bases— there could not be
a greater contrast in expectation:
one of black and white and gray–on–gray
the infant days of Jesus Television—

before the loaves and fishes; the water to wine.
And I sat there rocking to the gentle rhythm
of the you, and the me, and the bat, and the ball.
Tonight I return. This time from a pulse point

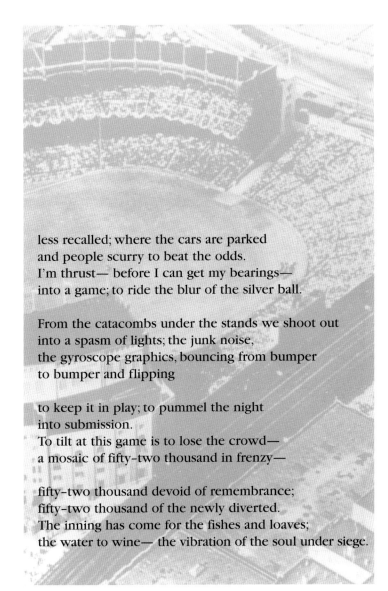

less recalled; where the cars are parked
and people scurry to beat the odds.
I'm thrust— before I can get my bearings—
into a game; to ride the blur of the silver ball.

From the catacombs under the stands we shoot out
into a spasm of lights; the junk noise,
the gyroscope graphics, bouncing from bumper
to bumper and flipping

to keep it in play; to pummel the night
into submission.
To tilt at this game is to lose the crowd—
a mosaic of fifty-two thousand in frenzy—

fifty-two thousand devoid of remembrance;
fifty-two thousand of the newly diverted.
The inning has come for the fishes and loaves;
the water to wine— the vibration of the soul under siege.

Two Lesbians Move In Next Door

The closing was a foregone conclusion:
they fell in love with the place.
Perhaps as they had with each other.
Though that took time to tell we're told.
And then with family to deal with and all:
parents, husband;
a couple of kids away at college.

The rain checks…
the reality checks.

Till one day when they were ready
diving headlong into the chilly surf.
As they no doubt will in their heated pool
done up in a Southwestern flair.

Overlooking the valley—
it cinched the deal.
The former residents had put it in.
Nice young couple. He a doctor;
she a nurse.
They met in surgery. Hernias, polyps;
outpatient sort of stuff.

I wonder which of the two
will throw out the garbage.
The one with short-cropped
graying hair
who seems to favor slacks,
and deals in mutual funds and stocks,
or the one who's been working on a script.

The Third Avenue El

Rail by rail
and girder by

arthritic girder
they tore it down.

Rivets as big as fists
undone—

the Great Monkey Wrench
of Progress.

And we had gathered
in the streets

the heart released
from tyranny

of darkness.
And sang "Noel."

And looked up laughing
faces to the sun

seeing it as though
for the first time.

What bit of it
there was before

had labored much
through latticed layouts

of tracks and ties
light then strobed

by rushing trains
on cabs and cars

on cobblestone.
How that chimera

had shimmied
and quaked

above our heads—
the stickball days

of sawed-off brooms
the ersatz bat

the strike zone chalked
upon the wall—

spilling sparks
and belching thunder

as if to proclaim
the Ironclad Nation.

Riders aloft in
the belly of the beast

would turn their gaze
through desperate windows

that gulped for air
in airless Augusts

to see men billowed
in boxer shorts

women wilting
in satin slips

mulling lives
in Hopper paintings.

It was commerce and art
for the price

of one Liberty dime.
Yet allegiance now

with the god of the sun
the chance to become

once again
invincible.

the LA river

        it trickles o

           ver a

              scroll

                of concrete

                    a

                   run-on

                      sentence a

                        leaking fountain

                                  pen

                            an end

an idea that

        never

           quite got started

      an idea

without

Smart Red Dress

Plastic covers on her couch
and on each of her chairs
the message was clear:

*Come looking for Johnnie
but don't get too comfortable
here.*

Equally pristine, the cream-
colored Cadillac casket
in which she was waked—

rosary beads in mother-of-pearl
winding across her hands—

she was and still remains:
the only corpse
in a smart red dress
that I have ever seen.

Cut just above the knee
it was the kind you might wear
to a dance

but far too informal for heaven:
a Wings & White Tie affair.

Perhaps, a touch of the devil's
designer hand here at play?

A heart attack.

One that by some odd chance had missed
her chain-smoking husband
who clung to her drapes
long after she had thrown him out.

She was the first mother of a friend
to go.

We, the rooster boys on the corner
reaching for those unreachable chords—

her Johnnie sang lead;
I backed him up.

And now that he is
the first of us to go—
like mother like son—
she reappears
the moment I hear.

As though if life begets life
the cord is somehow retied through death.

Or maybe it's just
that dress.

Jackie On Third

The whites of his eyes
like Martian moons;
dancing on fire
down the third base line.

The ice of a thief
who can pick a heart cold—
rob the crowd
of its maddening thunder.

The scent of a shark
who can smell blood or a balk
at 90 feet away
in the small fish of a toss.

Who steals home
in a goddamn World Series?
Only a man of frost, aflame
forced to swim against his pride.

Jackie In Central Park

She'd walk the park with Templesman—
A pair of doves as days grew pale.
They tried to catch the dying sun.

Dark glasses, a hat— she hid within fashion,
Yet each head would turn to mark her trail.
She'd walk the park with Templesman.

All threads of nonchalance undone—
The Celebrity Watcher's Holy Grail—
They tried to catch the dying sun.

Women with strollers and errands to run
Passed that point where the sailboats sail.
She'd walk the park with Templesman.

One final turn one Friday at one,
In hansom cab passing— a man once hailed.
They tried to catch the dying sun.

A prince in return, whose heart she had won
In the days of legend and musical tale.
She'd walk the park with Templesman;
They tried to catch the dying sun.

The California Sun

Everlasting, ever in our faces
like some catechism lesson
it's as numbing a presence as its counterpoise would be.
Say, the constant trickle of a mindless rain.

That some would lay themselves bare
to a devil's eye that seers the flesh—
fools that they are for daring to adore
that which never asked for their love—

it's the flowers who are the children of the sun.
Once it carved out a phosphorescent river
that ran through the jungle of the bleakest soul.
Once it ushered in the squire's heart,

where a dragon's den of darkness lay;
adventures in the young man's game.
A rebirth in every young man's spring
we threw time at the beast of dying.

We turned to the sun at every turn
as if denying that the clock would ever run dry.
As if these tales would not one day be retold
in the lunar terrain of our faces.

snow

we need to have snow
to see silence
in the making

each flake falling

       a hush

on city drums

Woodstock: 35 Years After

It's not as if I expected to find hippies
still trying to find themselves
        and/or
magic mushrooms
here in Woodstock
35 years after.

Yet, it's not as if
I didn't find any either.
Hippies that is.

Though the mushrooms
the magic
the mayhem remain

on some all points bulletin— missing.
Don't trust anyone over 60!

But despite all distillations
        this place
is still one in which to be lost and found
if one is to be lost and found at all.

Or to steal some pennies from a phrase well coined:
"Everything Old Age is New Age again."

Woodstock Nation— note the absence
of a *Starbucks*. And cell phones
are off the radar
rendered mute.
The "Sounds Of Silence" of Paul Simon swelling
in your very ears.

Woodstock Nation:
if they were any more laid back
they'd fall over. And not notice
the change in 90°
to the left.

Woodstock Nation:
where they see no rush to serve
        their fellow man.
Unless of course it be something spiritual
on the menu. Food can wait.

In fact heaven can wait.
Which ironically is the name of this food service place:
Heaven. I'm in *Heaven.*

And somewhere a salad is growing.

This being the only possible
        explanation
for it's not having arrived as yet. Yet, no hurry.

I'm only 58.
Four-hundred-six in dog years— and told
I do look much younger. Thank God.
In Heaven.

So go with the flow
though goes the flow
like melting fudge.
Yet dare not begrudge

the onanistic seeds
of the Flower Children
and now their children

still trying to take hold in Mother Earth.

VII. La Famiglia

"They sat on the stoop with paper fans and orangeades. They made their world. They said, Who's better than me?"

Don DeLillo, *Underworld*

Winter Street

He seems an apparition of the snow:
a whitewash of man and after-man—
a piece of business with the world unsettled.
With knotted brow and knitted tie—
he returns.

Ornery flakes swirl about him like bees—
he pays no notice; shows no trace
of wear for the distance he has come.
And with feet so determined toward this destination
his eyes seem unaware of a place in transition:
      the rabble of storefront signs
            in new alphabets— hand painted;
      the butcher, who held scraps for the dog,
          is gone;
      the candy store and sarsaparilla
pastry shop and charlotte russe—
gone to where sweet dreams go.

We tried to send you off with them
but you keep finding a way back
in those flimsy shoes so laughable—
on this journey in particular—
yet now I wear them every day too.

Does this satisfy you? Or shall
we meet here next time
            in a steely rain
pounding atop our heads unbowed,
so proud, so crowned with thorns.

Fire 'Scapes (Circa: Summer '59)

Zigging, zagging, clinging, flagging
      skeletons
           black bones
               of iron,
out of the closet for all to see;
      an affront
           to "Uptown"—
               parasites, yet
ready to quickly metamorphose for thee
      and offer
           on track
               deliverance
from an infernal death sentence,
      a trial by fire
           an Everlasting Hell
               at zero hour
when the flames are emphatic and before
      the first peel
           of a firehouse
               bell.
But until then, a holding tank
      for house plants
           matted mops
               thick mason jars;
a rack for sun-drying Sicilian hot peppers,
      and snipers nest
           for guttersnipes
               young gunners
heedlessly slinging Coca Cola caps at cars.

Second Hand Smoke

In a river of harangue
the street still flows
from the mouth of this upwardly mobile man.
Words with "K's" meant to cower; to kick
the air into silent submission.

Was it the father— a round of scotch
on his breath spewing forth
a propane fire
though yellowed teeth
set in a face of sandpaper— was it he

who first taught this lesson?
Or was it the whole birth
from their cauldron of malcontent
as it bubbled to overflowing
in that cubby hole of a flat?

Between the cavalcade of *Camels*
and the vapor of alcohol—
the wonder that it did not all
go to combustion. Or perhaps it did.
And I am now the blackened angel

that rose from the ashes
to fight new demons
in this world of matchbook enlightenment;
of Surgeon General warnings.

To They Who Leap Of Faith

for my children

I saw you go over the top
and down into the abyss—
the soles of your feet
left me behind.

Deeper you plunged
to where dragons still breathe fire;
sea lions in prismatic waters
you come up not for air
but for a charge of pure white light
then continue— flex in a void
within echo of the rigid ground
in which I pitch my iron staff.

I would have followed you
in the eternal summers;
a lemming with flaxen hair
cropped close to my thoughts
on hero and heaven—
I would have followed you who are both.

And you would have known me,
and seen me, and I— you,
in places that we cannot meet now
but perhaps will one day
when I tire of my vigil.

Naming Names

Racoots took numbers in "9-11"
a Bar & Grill on Roosevelt Street.
Healthy, at five-after-two would drop by.
Joe Patch and *Ribs* would come by still later;
Blackie scowling in the corner.
Johnny 5, who owned the place
and *Mooskie, Racoot's* competition
would talk about how close *Fat Anna* came
to hitting the Daily Double.
Willie Diapers stayed away
preferring *Mootchie's* on Market Street.
Garibaldi and the *Chillie* brothers
were always in the joint doing time.
Millionaire Red, didn't have "two sticks
to rub together." *Tommy Yum*:
forever making U-Turns in his '55 "Caddy"—
his brother *Yanno* didn't even drive.
Meanwhile *Rocky Nails* and *Tommy Cork*
hung out on James Street with *Pete the Greek*
and *Big Pete*— though *Petey Red*
opted for the 6th Ward on Mulberry Street
where *Tiger Rose* ranted and raved on the stoop.
It sent *Julia Mush* to Catherine Street near *Honey's*.
Lefty Guns with black and pattened leather hair—
the movie "Donnie Brasco" based on him—
shot up *Dapper's* club while he was gone.
See, *Sixie* was sexual with *Nicky Rat*.
Yet he never laid a hand on *Frankie Teets*
who became a cop. He liked to eat
at *Beanzie* and *Day-Day's* luncheonette
and owed *Mikey Shits* and *Matto* money.
And no one wanted to fuck with *Joe Scar*.
Frankie Balls might have been his only friend.
Frankie Black had one too many. Including
Louie Hood— whose corpse the cops found in a hall
next door to where *Johnnie Jupitor* lived
across from *Billy Gar Ding Ding*— who went ape shit
whenever you called him, as he called it, "The Name."
Louie Chisel Chin would calm him down.
Tommy Hunch, a midget, barely reached
the pedals of his big-finned car.
And *Va Cah-Cah* ("Go take a shit")
had an Olds in which he drove the guys
to Sheepshead Bay that night for clams.
I— *Pee Wee*— something told me: "Don't go!"
lived to carve their names in stone.

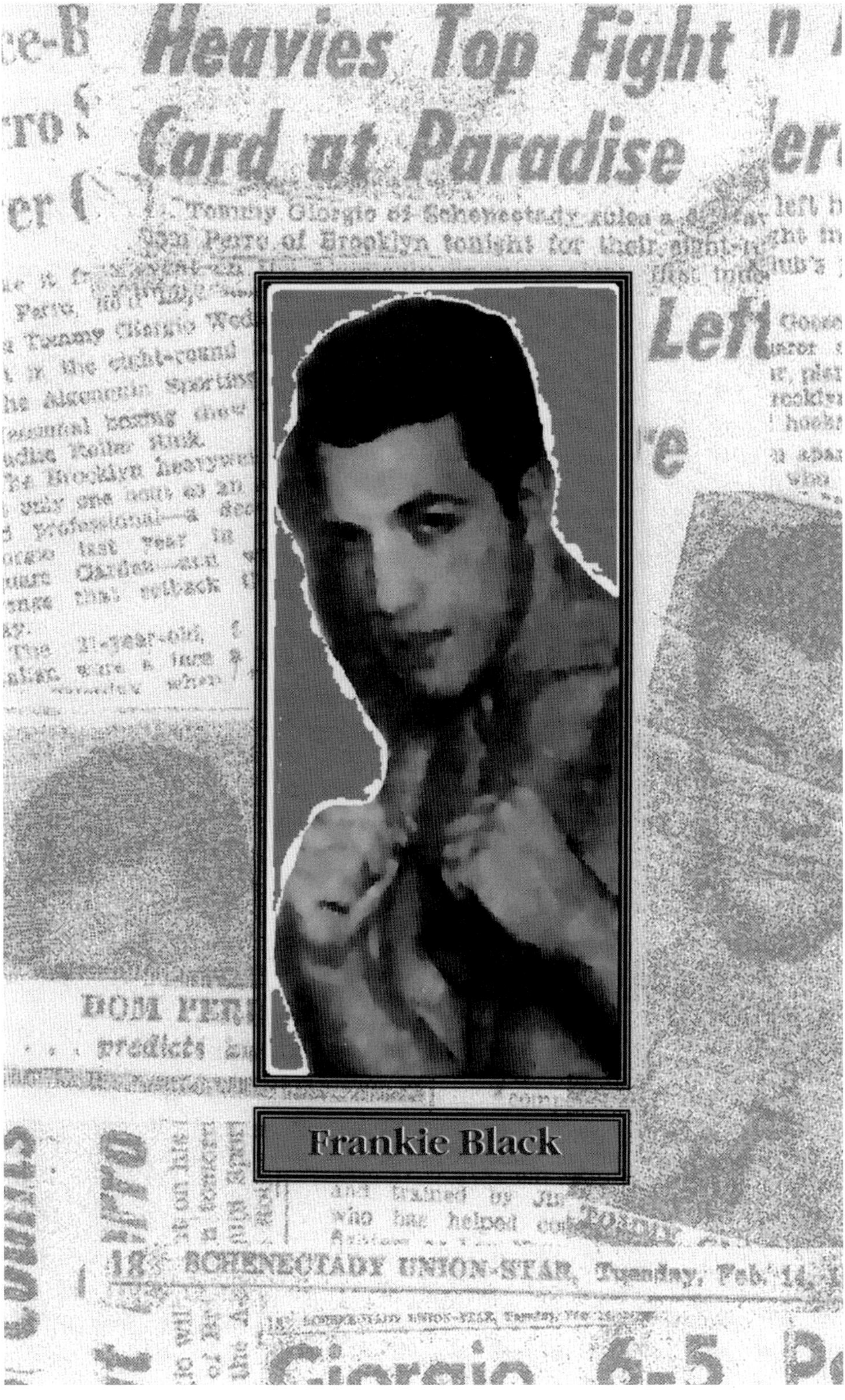

Frankie Black

Alliteration

It took me four years to paint like Raphael,
but a lifetime to paint like a child.

Pablo Picasso

When I read that
"energetic Eric eats electricity"—
the alliteration

the concept
meandering in blunt pencil
across wide-lined paper—

all but consumes me.
Does: "shimmering Sammy swallow stars"?
It would follow.

And I can do neither:
eat electricity
nor swallow stars.

From my darkest gardens
I might, if pressed,
muster a few fireflies. In this room,

the musty primers,
the smoke of learning,
mingle in my throat.

I need air.
I need water.
I need that which I used to float upon.

One day
it will eat *him*
swallow *him* whole.

Then he won't so much as
go near a toaster;
screw in a light bulb;

light up the sky.
I can in my role
As *Father Figure, fathom*

these *filament futures.*

Out Back

The hamster died
my son is sad.
He's seven and sad
can't sleep
eyes trickling
a virgin spring.

That's the thing about pets:
THEY DIE ON YOU.
COUNT ON IT.

Then send them off
to made-up heavens,
proper burial grounds—
the "closure thing."
Very important.
Very important.

Out back
the tiny tombstones multiply.
The hamster
next to
the goldfish.
The goldfish
next to
the goldfish next
to the goldfish
beside the frog
alongside
the parakeet.
It said "Hello."

This menagerie
that we cover up
with dark dirt:
with white lies—
only
the cat would have
no part of it;
too big
too resistant
to shallow graves.
Can you spell
eu-tha-na-si-a?

I did the honors;
drove the thing off
to the vet. Will they
remember?
What *will* they remember?
Take with them?
Hold on to

like their tattered bears—
splitting seams,
bald-patched fur,
a lost button or two—
who will nevertheless
survive us all?

When like the cat
they cart us away:
too big
to bury
out back?

Daughter Doodles While Away At College

Surely there must be something more
that warrants at least a Capitalization
of Environment and Humankind 101.
And it could be this; profoundly this:

THAT PIGS ARE TAKING OVER THE WORLD.

The environment a sty? Not a stretch.
Given the stench of false pretense for war.
Though maybe she meant to reference "The Waste Land":

Unreal City,
Under the brown fog of a winter dawn,
A crowd flowed over London Bridge, so many...

pigs! pigs! pigs! Yes of course.

That bridge stretched over the Charles this winter
she writes or rather doodles from Boston.
A place in January only Frost could love
if he weren't so busy in the fields
picking up loaves of stone for "Mending Wall."
(To please the yelping pigs of course).

Pigs, pigs everywhere
they vary their slop to stink.
It is we who must save our bacon.

"We" as in "Humankind" reduced to Rock reference:
at the off-center of it all, John Lennon.
He'd have shown these pigs to Yoko.
They knew squalor when they saw it;
they knew doodles when they made them.
Then had them signed and framed and up for sale.

So, I'll keep this one for such a time
that the pigs come grumping at the door;
and daughter battles while away at Carthage
in need of something supportive from home.

The Halloween Pageant

Swallowing that little chair
with the girth of your homemade turnip costume
you sit while the parade mulls about in assemblage—

a mess of pirates, ghouls, common thieves—
awaiting their call to dastardly deeds.
What have we done to you my son?

We saw nothing but the uniqueness and whimsy in it.
But these are not whimsical times— no not when
young men are being tried and tested.

Can you ever forgive us my son?
In your yoke and latex and swaddling cloth
you might for all the world still be

suckling at your mother's breast.
You ought be out there taking no prisoners
instead of alone with your shame and tears.

But don't worry my son, I will not let them
see you parade past them, in this way.
The mockery should have ended long ago back there

when they cast their lots for your clothes;
when they filled your mouth with gall.
I will kill any heathen who comes your way.

Come off your chair; I'm taking you home.
I'll make you a monster. I'll bring you back.
Then they'll see. Then they'll see.

Over the dog's head
hangs a wide leaf wet from rain.
He sniffs. Unconcerned.

Chihuahua: a dog.
Haiku: a poem. Given, both
much understated.

The Shed

If you gave him enough rope
he would tie up the world:

branch by branch;
stick by stick

each twig reconciled—

the immigrant sparrow reconstructing a nest
reconstructing a garden
where plants were not pastime,
but food in contention.

The leafy legumes, for example,
tattered with bullet holes
the work of gangster rabbits.
Or the cherry trees looted
by crows.

It went on this way for almost a century:
planting, tying, outfoxing nature.
Each maneuver, a snippet; almost unnoticed;
the old man, his old world...
reconstructing, reconstructing.

So that when young men
of no lineage—
just muscle and tools—
came to cart it away
it took them an eternity
to cut down and dismantle,
the small shed he left behind.